AF405311

Reading this stunning book of poems by Felicia Mitchell, I feel like a child released from the confines of a well-manicured lawn. Mitchell's Trail Magic allows me to wander freely (in my mind's eye) through the wild places that many of our fellow creatures call home. Even the titles of these gorgeous poems are enticing: "A Love Poem for My Son at Wilburn Ridge" (so poignant and one of my favorites) and "Birding at the Salt Wells, Saltville," to name a few. And while the poems in this exquisite collection are, in part, odes to the natural world, they are also the multi-layered, nuanced, and superbly crafted work of a skilled writer. Spending time with Mitchell's magical and deeply moving poetry is like walking wilderness trails with a naturalist—one who knows not only the names of every bird and flower but also the innermost workings of the human heart—her own as well as the hearts of others.
—Terri Kirby Erickson, *Night Talks: New & Selected Poems*

The magic of Felicia Mitchell's Trail Magic lies in the healing enchantment she finds on southwestern Virginia pathways and occasionally trails farther afield. In "Landscape with Shoes, Stewarts Creek," she writes: "Not much lasts, not the sound of water rushing/or a vireo singing in a tree whose name I'll forget/before I forget why I wanted to remember it all." Transience, uncertainty, self-awareness—all stated humbly yet wisely amid the bolstering presence of the natural world. Again, at this creek: ". . . the leaves, the twigs, the mud, the grass,/ skin and bones inside a simple pair of shoes." Mitchell's poems pulse with empathy for the vulnerable. After rescuing a creature from bike tires on the Creeper Trail, she reflects: "The millipede may not know to be grateful,/ the course of its life its own mystery." But we can be grateful for the fertile habitat of this poet's mind as she traverses a particular place.
—Suzanne Stryk, *The Middle of Somewhere: An Artist Explores the Nature of Virginia*

The poems in Felicia Mitchell's Trail Magic are decidedly more existential than in previous collections. As is consistent in her writing, though, these are poems of a hiker, someone who has spent a life connected to the natural landscape. As a reader, I am suspended within this vital landscape as the narrator of the poems ponders the complicated vicissitudes of growing older. As many writers turn to nature to reminisce or find symbolic meaning, Mitchell's poems demonstrate a life lived within the landscape among the community of birds, etc. Existentially, the life of a hiker usurps the dilemma or search for meaning. Within the landscape is a brightness of being—a profundity of now. I am so moved by this work of poems. As a hiker myself, I feel so connected through them.
—Jim Harrison, Director of Outdoor Programs and Semester-a-Trail, Emory & Henry University

TRAIL MAGIC

Trail Magic

Felicia Mitchell

Wising Up Press

Wising Up Press
P.O. Box 2122
Decatur, GA 30031-2122
www.universaltable.org

Cover art by Brigitte Natalie McCray, "Landscape," 2023, used by permission of the artist

ISBN: 979-8-9915552-0-3

Catalogue-in-Publication data is on file with the Library of Congress.
LCCN: 2024949148

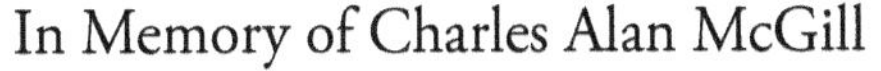

In Memory of Charles Alan McGill

CONTENTS

I

As Magical as a Single Life

THE ALCHEMY OF BIRD NESTS

I cremated hers with her,
the nest my mother carried
from one home to the other,
memento of her first nest:
a concrete block house
on an isolated road
where she loved my father,
gave birth to three babies,
and only moved to town
to a duplex beside a creek
because she needed a phone
with a fourth baby coming.

And now, walking in the woods,
by a house where I live alone,
I have found my own bird nest,
a wren nest I will treasure
in the same silver bowl
that held my mother's nest.
Small and twigged, ordinary,
it is as magical as a single life,
this nest, my mother's clipped hair
woven through it like veins.

BIRDING AT THE SALT WELLS

I hear a bird I have never heard before today.
Later I see one flitting in a thicket by the pond,
a warbler that looks like Buson painted it
with quick brushstrokes while composing a haiku.
In the water, Canada geese with goslings
glide near mixed mallards in variable colors.
It is almost summer, no gadwall in sight.
But there is a young man on a bicycle who pauses
to ask me where I am from, which people do,
and so I say "from here," waving my arm,
praising the birds, the trail, Food Country—
and then I ask the man if he has ever seen a bear.

He has seen deer, birds, has not seen no bear.
The roads are too close to the trail, he says,
so I wave my arm at the mountain across the valley
and observe that they must all be up there.
Later, an old man who has parked an old Ford
with an Obama-Biden sticker near the trail
to walk the dog somebody dropped at his house
four years before, a good dog that likes to get muddy,
tells me that once he saw five deer cross the trail.
I take that as an invitation to ask him about bears,
after I answer his question about where I am from,
my Mitchells from South Carolina, I say,
no relation to his next-door neighbors I do not know.
The old man has heard tell of bears but not here,
not on this trail by the salt wells where I,
I remind myself while I talk with the old man,
should be thankful for the company of birds.

Later, I will learn that I saw a yellow warbler.
This is the sort of bird that belongs on a life list,
so I make a note of it and also write "no bears."

DOWN BY THE RIVERSIDE

I laid down my burden down by the riverside
just as a black bear appeared in the pasture
where I had been counting sheep,
sheep that safely grazed while the bear stood,
tall, staring, listening to me singing a hymn
as if I were waiting to watch a preacher emerge
to dip me in the Holston like a penitent
instead of waiting to see what the bear would do—
and then it did what bears do, ambled on,
up the hill and through the brush away, away—
by then, I had stopped singing, the only holy need
I had gone with the bear across the hill,
the sheep dog silent in the field white as a holy ghost.

EVENING WALK, SMYTH CHAPEL ROAD

Weeds on the side of the road
are parched, the cows need water.
I find one in a patch of mud,
nuzzling a drainage pipe
the way a calf pulls at a teat.
Her calf is so very small.
The cow needs water to make milk.
It is so hot this month
that even wild berries are slow.
I look for signs of raspberries
and find wineberries growing
on the side of the mountain
where I always climb to pick them
in my rain boots from Target,
protection against poison ivy.
Eyeing the early wineberries,
looking for signs of raspberries
and blackberries as I turn back,
and finding so little growth,
I realize that the bag in my pocket
I always carry on these walks
may not be needed this year.
I may not pick a single berry
even when they ripen, if they do,
up and down Smyth Chapel Rd.
I will leave them for the birds.

MOCKINGBIRD, SMYTH CHAPEL ROAD

The color of asphalt,
this mockingbird blends in
like a berry stain on my bruise.
And he is frozen, too,
the way a deer would be,
in bright headlights,
but it is not light that startles.
It is the uncertainty
this side of the nest,
grass and tree lost for now,
for this twilit moment,
which feels too long.
The whole road feels too long.
Human, I stand there with him,
a shadow of a bird's frailty
except we are both strong.
So I will stand here with this bird
until two trucks pass
and night begins to fall some more
and the mother mockingbird
flitting and fussing above us
on the utility line
gets through to the little bird
with her bird language
in a way I cannot with words.
Only it is not a competition.
I do what I do, and I walk on,
berries in my grocery bag,
as the gray bird chooses green.

ODE TO SKUNK CABBAGE

Oh, harbinger of spring,
emerging from this earth
almost like Cupid's arrow
with a point to open hearts—
but more like a flower
that has waited all winter
to peep up from the earth
through brown leaves or snow
just as the sun promises
to come a little closer
to a Valentine like no other—
this one and only earth—
to warm us up, once again.

SMYTH GAP

Some mornings, I walk until the asphalt ends
and a rooster crows.
And then I walk a little farther down the road,
past a house somebody is tearing down,
slowly, as if nobody will want this site.
Every year, something disappears: doors, windows,
lately the shingles on the roof.
How long until there is nothing there
but an unkempt gap in a gap in Walker Mountain?
It is cooler here in winter and summer,
as shaded and as guarded as a holler.
This is where I find both berries and Christmas trees.
This is where bears sleep or hunt
or stumble into the Garden of Eden
at the foot of the mountain
on a midnight stroll.
I look for bears up the side of the hill,
even when I know they are hibernating.
I hope for them when they are not.
I am never afraid.
I know the crows will let me know
if ever I should turn around.
I know I have never feared anything here,
not even an altercation I witnessed
between two people screaming at each other
on the porch of the disappearing house.

SUGAR HOLLOW

There was an afternoon
a murder of crows
murdered a wood duck—

though there was no malice,
so maybe it was not murder
but hunger for food

instead of hunger for malice.
I watched from the hill,
not expecting the ending.

I was looking for ducks,
and heard crows overhead,
but by the time I got to the pond

the crows were starting to eat
the wood duck on the ground.
It was not even dead.

In times like these,
you just have to walk away
and let nature be

even as the brilliant blue
of a wood duck's feather
sticks in mind like flint on flint

when the world bursts into flame
with every sad thing that ever happened
to the frail and the faltering.

WILD GRAPES NEAR SALTVILLE

Sometimes I have to pick the grapes
growing on a train trestle near Saltville
across from the Superfund site,
and I have to eat them too,
as if they are all there is to eat.
And maybe they are all there is to eat
on a Sunday afternoon in summer
so many birds removed in time from soldiers
who dug salt nearby, for the war, that war,
and even more birds and deer removed in time
from woolly mammoths that roamed here,
right here where I can pick grapes
and eat them too, grape by grape,
as I watch a turkey fly across the fence
and land there, there where grass grows
where once so many chemicals spilled
that fear fell off our trees like acorns.

The people whose land this was,
before us—before the factory workers,
the farmers, the soldiers with bayonets—
would have picked the grapes and eaten them,
without thinking about toxic chemicals
or how I would one day be here too,
picking grapes as if there is no tomorrow
and thinking there might be no tomorrow.
These people would have eaten the grapes.

WHAT ANSEL ADAMS TAUGHT ME

A black and white rainbow
is as colorful as a colored rainbow
drawn with a child's crayons
because when its light hovers
inside a photograph for years—
like an emanation, an incarnation—
its spectral moment is present,
never past and never future.
Even without the word "rainbow,"
I would see a rainbow here
as it arcs across a waterfall,
the layering of light against water
shining through a hundred years
and one glass picture frame.
Without color mediating,
even manipulating, I meditate,
neither here in the museum
nor there on the rock with Adams—
hiking nowhere but inside a brain
infinite as time if I let myself let go
of where I am supposed to be
and what I am supposed to see.

II

Distracting Me from Myself

AFTERNOON AT ALVARADO

Sometimes a walk
is both a vigil
and a requiem,
a white bloodroot
emerging from its leaf
as much a reminder
of how life cycles
as a sign of spring—
bloodroot petals are
as precious as tears.
Hepatica blooms in rocks
living colonies, roots enmeshed
the way friends
end up friends for life,
their stories intermingling.
Hiking with a group of friends
on a Tuesday afternoon
can feel like church
when one who is missing this hike
out of so many hikes together
feels as present as a phoebe calling
from a tree in the woods.
"For where two or three
are gathered together,"
Jesus said, "there am I too
in the midst of them."
Today we gathered like that,
my friends and I, needing
to be in the midst of the divine
and each other too,
when communion was as natural
as the air we breathed.

ASTERS IN AUTUMN

I was here
and you were here
and you are gone
and I am here
and the asters bloom
in the late early autumn
afternoon, purple,
like circles under my eyes
or a vein pulsing
in your hand.

IN ONE SITTING

Jefferson National Forest

A beaver long gone
now works to move the water,
its limb over rocks.

Nestled in the twigs,
a plastic water bottle,
too blue to forget.

Over my shoulder,
a white rhododendron blooms.
At my feet, busy ants.

Wind has blown petals
onto the matted pine needles,
tears of joy on flushed cheeks.

Through sky and branches,
the sun finds one perfect leaf
and rests with a fly.

The creek runs away,
leaving the mountain for river.
Rain will take it home.

Little rocks, big rocks,
rocks hidden by the water,
rocks sunning like toads.

Above my cloister,
a helicopter passes,
louder than a bee.

Water, gray and white
and green and brown and silver—
colors from the sun.

I almost killed it,
the mosquito on my hand,
then I changed my mind.

Moss like strokes of paint
on a brown, earthen palette
is still wet with rain.

Roots are more exposed
than I am here, on my rock,
apart from the path.

Some of these tall pines
are much younger than I am, and some
older than I'll ever be.

SHOWY ORCHID

There was just the one,
so I sat with it by the creek.
We knew each other then,
the way old friends do
or relatives, when young
and not yet estranged
or old and ready to reconcile.
Above us, a vireo sang.
Near the creek, on a rock,
a snake rested in the sun.
It was entirely peaceful,
my time with the showy orchid.
The violet-pink of this flower
reflected an amethyst in my ring,
the amethyst wishing it was wild.
A swallowtail butterfly, sensing that,
lit in my finger for a moment.
I buried the ring by the orchid.
Maybe I wished I was as wild,
or maybe I wished I were tamer,
but I knew I needed a ring
no more than the showy orchid
needs a crystal vase.
And we sat, a breeze blowing,
and I drank some water
that I shared with the orchid
before I set back up the trail.

STRAIGHT BRANCH

There was an afternoon in the forest
when all the fungi I passed were white,
and all the ferns beside the trail were green.
In the sky, gray storm clouds gathered,
but it never did rain or storm that afternoon
when the sun came out suddenly in a blue sky,
shining on ironweed growing in the meadow,
ironweed as purple as the goldenrod was yellow.
The rain jacket I was wearing was also purple,
and my shoes were as brown as dirt,
but my spirit was clear, like water from a spring
trickling down the branch of a mountain creek.

LESSON, BIG LAUREL CREEK

If there are steps leading to the creek,
take them, one by one,
until you stand right next to the water.

Even if the beavers have already built,
you can pretend this could be your home,
this stretch of land between woods and water.

I would put my house on the rock in the middle.
I would make it out of fallen limbs and river glass,
with curtains made of scarves hikers have lost.

Beavers would be my neighbors, and bears,
and bobcats too would drink the same water
that I drink and bathe and swim in.

In the spring, when laurels bloom,
I would pull blossoms and stick them in my roof
the way I used to stick them in my hair.

In summer, I would bask in the sun on the rock
until the sun set over the mountain
and everybody wondered where I had gone.

By fall, I would probably get lonely for my other house,
the one on the other side of the mountain.
with a fireplace and running water and a bed.

I could walk there from here, back up the steps,
come winter, if I knew my key would still work
and my cat would still remember me.

NEUROMODULATION

An app trains my ears
not to mind the ringing,
or is trying to best it can,
but when I hear crickets
singing by the creek,
the sound of the water
as peaceful as silent ears,
I laugh and say to my friend:
this is what I want,
for the sounds in my head
to sound like this, just this,
like these crickets and that creek
on a late-summer day—
even the occasional call
of a killdeer breaking through
the shimmer of crickets
and alto of a creek running.
If I can will myself to hear that,
instead of the ringing—
a dreadful drone that lulls me—
I know I will not go crazy
or fall asleep late afternoon,
the way I do now, in a chair,
unless I put in my ear pods
and listen to sounds dancing
from neuron to neuron,
distracting me from myself.

MILLIPEDE

This millipede on a bicycle trail
has no notion of eternal life,
no arrogance that its 60 feet
can outpace 60 humans.
It could take an hour to cross
or not cross at all, just fall there,
not so much a victim of a wheel
(because all wheels do is spin,
without vengeance or vindication)
but just a millipede getting run over.

The death of a millipede is not a tragedy.
All a millipede does is crawl,
no sense of urgency or eternity.
It does what millipedes have done
for centuries in these mountains,
even with bicycles in its path.
I, on the other hand, or foot,
am a kindred spirit out rambling.
I do not need a bike to move
or get in touch with my primal cells.

The wildflowers are enough to lift me,
their colors all the stained glass I need.
Bloodroot hides its red rhizomes
under the freshly thawed earth,
its flower white as a first communion.
Perhaps I brood as much as a human might,
but I feel kinship with this millipede on the trail,
the difference between us small and large.

Mighty today, towering over something small,
I pick this millipede up gently in my hand
and carry it across the bike trail
before the next wave of cyclists flies by.
The millipede may not know to be grateful,
the course of its life its own mystery.
Even so, the world needs more millipedes,
when it is spring, in the mountains, in Virginia.

THE TATTOO I DID NOT GET

Bloodroot sends up leaves,
angel wings on earthen flesh.
A flower comes next.

My right breast, hollow,
is the opposite of spring.
It has bloomed and gone.

I look for flowers
that grow on the sides of trails,
my path a journey.

My left breast likes sun,
flesh flushing as winter wanes.
Its nipple blossoms.

Where the sun falls first,
a bloodroot will bloom early,
its leaves a blessing.

I do not need ink
to replace what cancer took,
no nipple tattoo.

A scar is plenty,
its track like a bird's scratching
for something hidden.

A bloodroot roots deep,
even deeper than earthworms.
I kneel over it.

WHAT WASN'T THERE

I could see violets that were not there,
not yet, their leaves unfolding from a rock
still fringed with ice.
                       I could see bluebirds
that were there, circling bare trees in a thicket,
but there were no nests, not yet, birds scouting
for what they would need in time,
the way I was looking for what I would need
in time.
         On the edge of the river, trees teetered.
Beavers had been busy, and would be busy again,
late, when I was not there to see them.
                            Come spring,
I would return to this river without a coat.
Now I was there with a coat loose over my shoulders,
wanting to feel the cold that made me catch my breath
as much as I wanted to see sun working the soil.

III

Just Walking this Walk

APPALACHIAN TRAIL SOUTH

I lost the trail
while I stood on the trail,
leaves at my feet
unlike breadcrumbs.
I did not see the clues.
I saw only light
through open branches
and rocks and boulders.
I smelled winter
touching autumn
on its shoulders.
Time had caught me
and held me in its moment
the way a child is held
just out of the womb.
But just as I stood there,
startled by a fear
of stepping forward,
a raven called from overhead
and two men came
around the bend,
heavy with their packs.

"I lost the trail,"
I told them—the men, the raven—
rooted on the earth,
leaves at my feet
unlike breadcrumbs.
"This is the AT South,"
one man said,
gesturing at my feet,
at all the leaves,
and I said, "I know."
I knew where I was.
I just did not know
where I was.

CONTROLLED BURN, WHITETOP

The landscape feels different today,
as if I could be hiking on another planet
but one with air I can breathe.
Still, early spring after a morning rain
is as palpable as the chemical odor,
nature and nurture competing here
with a backdrop of blueberry bushes
and still bare hawthorn trees.
Somewhere under this ground,
the unwanted undergrowth all gone,
a Gray's lily has been spared.
Controlled burns are supposed to help.
Still, as if on less familiar planet,
I put one foot in front of the other foot
on the way to Buzzard Rock,
following the sound of a junco calling
from a cedar atop this charred earth.

LEWIS FORK WILDERNESS

Not all that glitters is gold.
Sometimes it is a rock
where frost has melted
but not evaporated yet,
sun bright, leaves without trees.
Seasons come and go.
Ferns know winter is near,
and the nest in the crook of a tree
is empty, bereft of feather.
The rock is enduring,
its season this moment.
It was always this moment.
Decades ago, farther up,
larger and rough as time,
the rock rolled or was thrown
or some earthquake picked it up
and dropped it here.
Now the rock is where it is.
It is what it is, a rock glistening
because the sun is shining
on a late fall afternoon.
When a junco calls out,
the empty nest replies.

LOOSE STRIFE, GRAYSON HIGHLANDS

It never comes in small packages,
only in bulk, like tea or heartbreak—

and it is as tenacious as a raven
circling the pinnacle of your life

while you stand there above it all
looking down at wildflowers

that would never be as pretty in a vase
as on top of that earthen grave.

A LOVE POEM FOR MY SON AT WILBURN RIDGE

If you were a wild pony,
you would be wilder than I am by now—
out there on the other side of the mountain
looking for a greener pasture
and your own mare.
You might be drinking water from a creek
at this very moment.
I would no longer be following you,
nudging you away from humans
who stand with cameras and smiles,
nudging you with the weight of my belly
as I turn a corner where we will climb.
I would not be writing a poem about you,
although I think I would recognize you
if our paths crossed on the mountain.

But you are a grown man and not a wild pony,
and I am not the old gray mare.
Still, I remember your own lithesome legs
and how they galloped up this trail
even as I trudged, a little slow, behind you.
You always knew I would be there,
not so far behind.
I always knew you would be up ahead,
not so far out of reach.

Years come and years go.
I am even slower now and alone,
a hiker who seeks the company of wild animals.
I return to this meadow once a year, son,
and watch the ponies with their foals.
I remember how it was.
Those were the days when I would follow you anywhere
even if the top of the mountain
was as high as Virginia got.
You remember how it was
when there was nothing but blueberries
at the end of our hike.

TEXTING WHILE HIKING

It does happen, sometimes,
the click of my fingers
alongside the clack of my feet
on a rocky trail,
just as it did the other day
crossing Buzzard Rock.
I am not ashamed to admit it.
Silurian, that rock—
so old, millions of years old,
it can ground me
and put everything
(or almost everything)
into perspective,
and not just the panoramic vista
with big, big sky.
Even texting while hiking across it
can feel like something ordained.
Keeping spirit in sync
with a friend far removed
in our life's journeys—
my feet taking up where his left off—
there is no judgment from sun
or sandstone or afternoon sky
when there is a way to seek each other's company
across the ages, across some rocks,
across the miles between us.

TRAIL MAGIC

Usually, it is somebody with cookies
who also brings cold milk
or something like that,
maybe hot chocolate instead of milk
or cake instead of cookies.
Sometimes it is a can of beer.
It is always something as ordinary as kindness.
Now and then, it is a wind caught in the rocks
that sounds like a whisper from your mother
in the midst of a hike as winding as her life.
On days like that, it is impossible not to stop in your tracks.
It is impossible not to wonder what is going on.
What is going on inside the rocks inside that cave?
Could there be another entrance into heaven?

High atop the rocks today, in late November,
one white round-lobed hepatica bloomed
as if spring had never come and gone,
as if winter was not days away—
the first snowfall already fallen.
I stopped in my tracks on the trail and studied it,
this flower as real as the day was short,
but when I lifted my camera to take a photo,
I lost my focus and had to step back
to search for it with naked eyes.
By the time I failed to get a photo,
the wind had stopped, the voice of my mother,
or the wind, drifting across the rocks
up the mountain into the sky.

WALKING TO GEORGIA

I do not need to get there,
one foot in front of the other
pushing me forward
while the pack on my back
draws me the other way.
With enough resistance
to spur me on, and on,
I can rock the rhythm
of these hills, these trails,
as if a heron that flew
from the pond below Beartree
will be my spirit guide
until I pass Damascus
and pick up a bear's tracks
through Tennessee.
Because I once knew an orchid,
I know there will be a bear,
just as surely as I know
what mushrooms not to eat
and where to pitch my tent.
Meanwhile, I walk this walk.
Each breath I take, laboring,
every breath I take, labored,
mountain air in my lungs,
I am as still as a millipede
running across a rock.
I am ready for the exhale.
I do not need to get to Georgia.
I do not need to carry Katahdin
on my back inside my pack.
I am just walking this walk.
I am not going anywhere.

YOUNG MAN ON THE APPALACHIAN TRAIL

I taught him the names
of a few things that afternoon,
things like spotted wintergreen
and flowering raspberry,
and he told me his trail name
and his real name too.
For a few miles, I was a grandmother,
walking with a young man
younger than my hiking shoes
and yet as wise a thru-hiker can be
when he is two states removed from home
and on his way to Maine.
Before we shook hands and parted,
he said he had not walked enough with me
to know my trail name
but I told him my real name
and wished him well,
there on the trail, and in life,
not knowing if I might see him again
or ever be able tell him my trail name,
if I ever earn it, Blue Daisy.

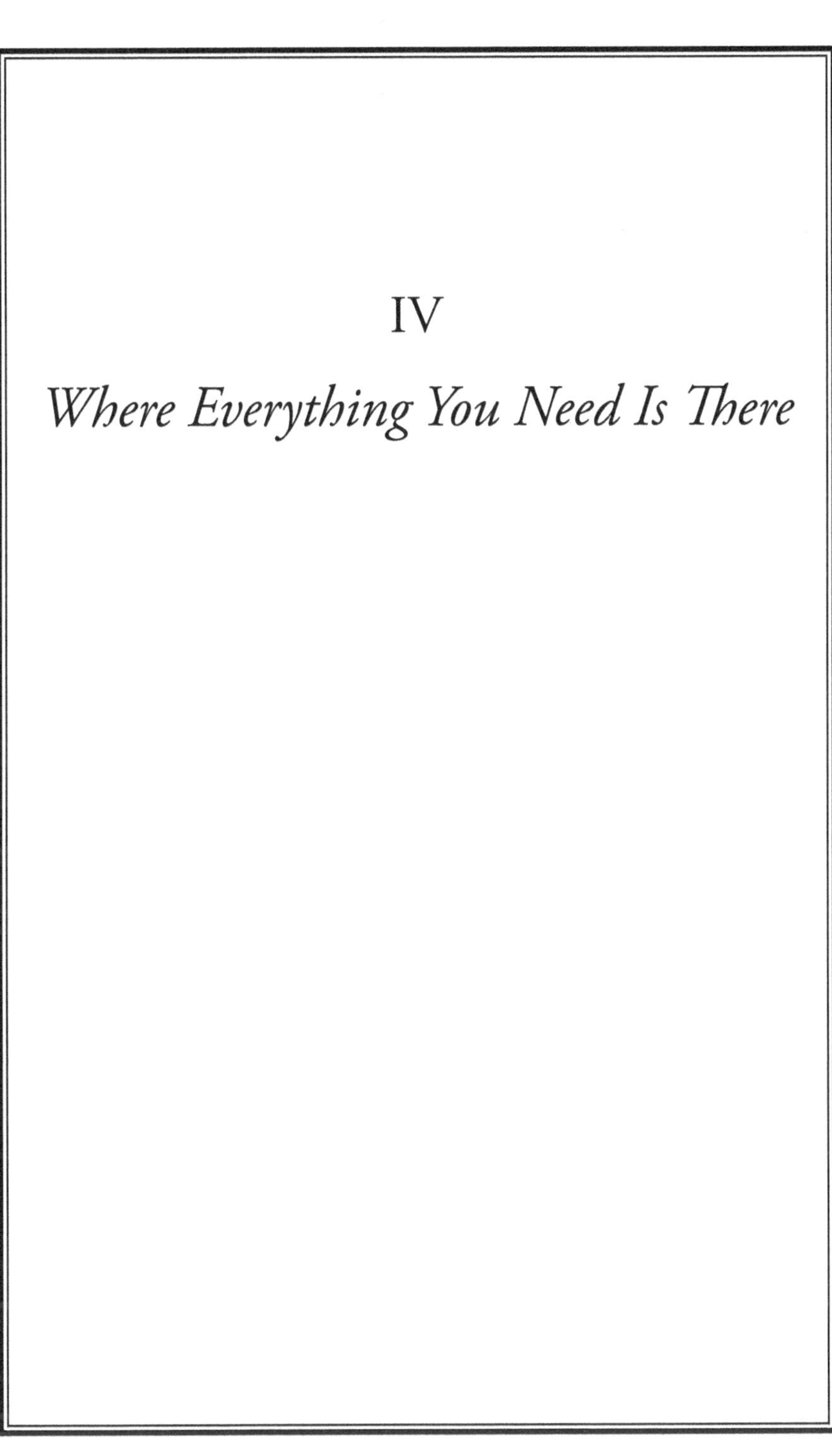

IV

Where Everything You Need Is There

BLUE-EYED MARY, MY OLD FRIEND

I would follow you anywhere,
from your yard to a bog,
from a bog to a mountain top.
Even to the place we call old age.
After more than 50 years,
I can think of us as little girls
traversing a mountain trail—
me for the first time
thanks to the kindness of
your kind-hearted parents.
I also think of us as old women
prepared to call ourselves old.

Remember how we once sat
and dug with our hands in the dirt,
looking for bits of garnet?
I still have mine in my jewelry box,
along with a ring you gave me
the afternoon we played dress-up.
At 66, we are both young and old.
Now when we get together,
we walk and study flowers,
a violet as precious as a friendship
when I see it through your hand lens.
Yesterday, seeing blue-eyed Mary
blooming for the first time in my life,
I wished you were there with me
in that meadow on Clinch Mountain.
I wanted to hear you exclaim *Collinsia verna*
as a chestnut-sided warbler sang overhead,

and so I did, in my own head,
you as much there with me when we are apart
as I am with anybody on this life's journey
when friends are as essential to a life
as fall and winter are to a spring flower
that will shed its seeds in summer
to prepare to start again, blooming,
always blooming, life cycles as constant
as a constant childhood friend.

BY THE CLINCH RIVER, ST. PAUL

I was looking for pawpaws
and found the pawpaws
but there were no pawpaws

so I listened to the birds,
some birds I did not know
and some birds I recognized
the way I would recognize
myself even before I was born.

By the river, an osprey called,
and then it flew and called again.
I watched it and listened again.
A coal train came down the tracks

so I paused in my own tracks
and watched it through the leaves.
There were so many pawpaws
and no pawpaws at all

so I kept walking down to the falls,
where I turned to pick up a walnut,
and there it was, the one pawpaw
I had been looking for but not finding,
blinded as I was by the trees.

Carrying my pawpaw back,
I knew sometimes one is enough.
One pawpaw, one morel,
one monarch sighting in a season.
One love as biodiverse as a river
where everything you need is there,
even one pawpaw, ripe as time.

FIELD PUSSYTOES AT LOVER'S LEAP

My toes are black with dirt,
but at least the footprints I tracked
down the side of the hill at Danville Pike
go right back up again.

I did not leap when I had the chance.
I decided on a slow crawl,
something like swimming against the tide
to reach my one pair of shoes
so I could walk through burning sand.
It was a barefoot Saturday afternoon.
And how blue was the sky?
As blue as a sky that opens its arms
to as many clouds it can handle.

If the sky was blue, the paint on the rocks
at Lover's leap, where I paused to walk,
was pink with initials and crooked hearts:
and the field pussytoes were white.

GENTRY FALLS

A bobcat stepped
on a rock by the creek,
its paw prints like a postcard
from paradise:
Step into this forest, the postcard said,
and savor all signs.
That was a sign,
and so were all the creek crossings,
a sign that we were inserting ourselves
into a scene out of a day out of a year
that knew too much mourning
back there, back in town.
Here everything was alive,
even everything that was dead—
even a decay pungent
with a scent of deep woods
smelled like hope.
And then on a tree by the falls—
so many initials carved by visitors
a tombstone but not a tombstone,
more like a totem pole,
one more sign.

LANDSCAPE WITH SHOES, STEWARTS CREEK

One day the wind will blow the leaves away,
and every twig away, and the dried mud,
or maybe time will turn it all to a fine dust:
even this grass as green as any patch of grass
and the black shoes that are stepping on it,
gingerly, avoiding trout lilies underfoot.
Not much lasts, not the sound of water rushing
or a vireo singing in a tree whose name I'll forget
before I forget why I wanted to remember it all:
the leaves, the twigs, the mud, the grass,
skin and bones inside a simple pair of shoes.

LIFE LESSON AT PANDAPAS POND

This is what I tell her:
There is always a bigger fish.
Sometimes one gets away.
The one we saw was big,
so I whispered to my friend
to look, fishers feet away.
Next to a colony of lily pads,
it did what crappies do.
I did what humans do.
Measuring it with my eyes,
I decided this creature was crafty
and as long-lived as artificial bait.
A voice from a biology lecture,
or else from some song,
reminded me how the strong survive.
Another voice in my head
told me that the fishers
were not there to catch the crappie
but simply to try for a few hours
until it was time to go home.
Who would truly get away?
The fish or the fishers?
When it was time for us to turn,
a tadpole about to hop swam by.
I wondered what it would like best:
the time in the pond, or the forest,
or the time in between,
in the water with wise old crappies
and better able to hide among lily pads
than it would be again for some time.
My friend just walked ahead.

LUNA MOTH

I found it on the trail,
caught between a rock
and a hard place—
you know that place.
I know that place too.
It is the reason I hike,
the reason I was there,
then, that afternoon,
by the James River,
looking for Balcony Falls
and finding a luna moth.

I picked the moth up,
thinking that no moth
should spend its last breath
(do moths have breath?)
alone on a mountain trail,
and carried it with me
until I was in the wilderness.
Mountain laurel bloomed.
galax bloomed, blueberries,
rattlesnake weed,
one wild pink azalea,
its petals falling into ferns.
Everything was blooming
that afternoon, except the moth,
which I lay inside a hollow log
on the side of the trail,
an autumn leaf its shroud.

This was not a sad occasion.
The luna moth had lived its life
in a world as green as breath.

MOURNING CLOAK AT PILOT MOUNTAIN

The serape draped across my chair back home
shares the colors of this butterfly on this path,
where I will stand for a few minutes watching it
before I take the time to identify it by its name:
Nymphalis antiopa, mourning cloak.
A harbinger of spring in mourning colors
is certainly not out of place on this February day,
a solitary hike the way I have chosen to mourn
my first love, my soulmate, a man who called me
just before today from far away to say farewell
before journeying to another place I will not join him,
at least not in my own lifetime, not on this earth.
What can rival a lifetime of loving someone?
I wanted to come to a trail I had never hiked,
to do something I had never done before,
and here I am seeing something I never saw,
a butterfly that makes me say "ah, ha!"
Later, when I look at the serape he wore
and then gave to me, something I kept close
for fifty years even as he was far away or farther,
I will see colors shapeshifting into a butterfly.
And if I drape the serape across my shoulders,
remembering the one who gave it to me,
I will perhaps feel as if I am lifting my wings
like a mourning butterfly or ageing earth angel
to join my wandering man of a soulmate,
wherever he has gone, this time, this last time.

POND MOUNTAIN WILDERNESS AREA

I crossed a creek 14 times
on my way up and again 14 times
on the way back down from Pond Mountain,
cold water sloshing inside my waterproof shoes
like new soles.

                    But it was the sun that washed me clean,
not the creek, its light dappling through rhododendron—
some rays falling on petals of trout lilies and trillium
and other rays falling on the scar on my chest
where I wore my shirt open, the t-shirt underneath
snug against my one breast.

                    Nobody sees the scar
underneath the t-shirt, its clean line so much neater
than the trillium-red scar where my port lay.

                        And
every time I find myself in the wilderness on a hike,
I forget that it is there, and every time I am stronger,
even strong enough to run down a trail in wet shoes
on a sunny afternoon not because a storm threatens
or I am afraid of bears but just because I can.

RACHEL WHEN I AM OLD

I want to be like Rachel when I am old,
and she is not even old yet in her seventies—
I just know that she will be the kind of old
that makes other women covet her strength,
the way some women in the nursing home
would stare in awe at my mother Audrey
when she stood up out of her wheelchair
to pour a cup of coffee from a pot.

Hiking yesterday at Wilson Creek,
some of us as sigogglin as the rocky trail,
we persevered because Rachel persevered
the way my mother persevered,
even when she forgot exactly how to walk
or think but awed us with her other skills.

One day, when I am less steady on my feet,
and still have my wits about me,
I want to go back to Grayson Highlands
and hike steep and rocky Wilson Creek Trail again
with the resolve Rachel showed yesterday
when it was summer with just a hint of fall,
red leaves at our feet mixing in with snakeroot
ripe with white blossoms attracting butterflies
and the rushing water in the creek swift as time.

V

In the Right Direction

BEYOND THE GARDEN WALL

Just past the old brick kitchen,
around the corner from a statue
—a golden statue of Dionysus—
lie two fallow rice fields,
fields where blackbirds sing
along with the ghosts of workers
sodden with mud, afraid of malaria,
women who worked dawn to dusk
to plant and harvest rice.
And there are replicas of rice trunks
to show how flooding was manipulated
to make a golden rice grow
as if Senegal was not a continent away.

You are supposed to stay on this trail
that meanders past antebellum history
alongside a creek with alligators
and great blue herons that eat fish
without minding that you are there.
Sometimes a wood peewee sings too
or a crow or a hawk looking for prey.
There are too many voices on this trail
for your mind to settle into a quiet,
the quietude of the contemplative.

Thoughts can nag more than mosquitoes.
They can make you fantasize about this trail
just beyond a garden wall
that might as well be a border between slavery
and what looked like freedom,
a freedom full of copperheads
and alligators and malaria
and an overseer with a long gun.
On a sunny day in early May,
just after you drink a glass of iced tea,
it is far too easy to traverse this history.
The hard part is not the heat.
The hard part is how easy it is for you, a tourist,
to put one sandaled foot in front of the other—
and just go anywhere she wants to go.

BRISTLE CONE PINE, COLORADO

Jesus, etched in bark,
is not smiling,
his eyes are sad.
Over his shoulder,
one eye watches.
Whose face is that?
It could be after,
the cross a halo.
It could be Jesus too.
It could be before,
cross as premonition.

These trees are so old.
Like clouds,
they invite speculation.
What you see in bark
is not always
what you see in bark.
The piney knot
could be an opening
to the womb.
The womb could be
a cave, an icon;
the cross, a sign
signifying birth,
not death.

Bark old as Jesus
is a mystery,
like the resurrection.
Trees with faces
have no concordance
other than
the mind,
the mind
on clouds.

CONGAREE SWAMP

I wanted to see a warbler,
any variety of warbler,
but all I saw was robins—
robins high in pine trees
and robins in the swamp
foraging for fruit and bugs.
I could hear the warblers,
their high-pitched voices
mixed within the robin calls,
and once I thought I saw one
picking its way around
a cypress stump in front of me
but that turned out to be a kinglet,
the golden crown of this songbird
startling amidst all the robins.

Robins have to live somewhere.
Yards are not big enough to hold them,
I know, but oh, I wanted to see a warbler,
one fairy of an unexpected bird
in a field of common feathers.

FLATIRONS

Each time I hike the Flatirons,
I meet a new challenge—
sometimes one my son assigns,
sometimes one that arrives
like an epiphany as I meander up
and decide to try something new,
something like scrambling across rocks
as far as I can scramble, safely,
such a meager achievement
in the big picture of Boulder's scene
(and yet a huge success for me).
Last time, on a new trail, I got lost,
the rocks I rested on another planet.
Every direction I looked?
It all looked like the same gray matter.
I could have used my phone.
I could have panicked and called my son.
But one thing I learned early on
is to leave early enough on a hike
to have time to find yourself before dark.
I also depend on voices I hear,
this time the voice of a young mother
carrying her toddler who paused with me
when I called out to her on her ascent
(opposite to my stalled descent).
She mothered me with a bandaid for my ankle
(scraped while walking in circles)
and pointed me in the right direction
before I ambled on down my rocky way,
waving farewell to her and her little boy.

GREAT WALL

There I was, stepping up, and up again,
the way I step up sometimes at work,
during lunch, up and down the halls
and up and down the stairs, until I am awed
at what a body can do when it tries to.
Sometimes, at work, at lunch, I walk briskly,
not attending to the walls or ceiling.
Other times, I want to stare at posters,
finding a landscape to insert myself into
on days that it is too cold to walk outside.
Truly it is never too cold to walk outside,
not where I live, even if it is close to 0
and the ground is crackling at my feet.
I own so many winter coats and pairs of boots.
But sometimes I just want to be indoors
when a walk through my workplace on a cold day
is nothing like a walk up the Great Wall.
That is what I was thinking of today, stepping up,
and up again, the fog I experienced in China
obscuring my vista now a continent away.

OCONEE RIVER, ATHENS

It has been a year now
since I saw a hawk
resting on a tree branch
overhanging the riverbank
while I walked at dusk
with an old friend who talked
about this bird and other hawks
and about kayaking the river

and about how brown water flows
from the Oconee to faucets in town,
pumped from a river's basin
into our mouths, into my mouth,
where it can be as hard to shape words
to describe a hawk on a riverbank
as it is to spot a red-shouldered hawk
perched in a tree by a river in a city—

but sometimes words flow
like a river and you find
a hawk resting there.

THE RIDGES CEMETERY NATURE TRAIL

They are pink and white petals on the Virginia springbeauty,
colors from summer dresses women might have worn
before they came here—or even then, even here,
their matching bonnets frayed but serviceable
on airings on the grounds of the asylum.
The pink and white stripes are also like welts or scars,
surprising against the pallor of tombstones
worn down by sorrow and age and acid rain.
They streak across the grass below the asylum,
striking in their insistence on remaining wild.
It is clear nobody ever treats the lawn,
with violets and dandelions emerging too
from this sad and hallowed soil.
I think a soldier who never went home from war
once wept, his scars wet with holy water,
to see these flowers growing by the woods.
He would have lain down and let his tears fall
into their roots until he forgot he was human.
I think a woman from the hills would remember stories
of how to eat springbeauty corms like potatoes
or how to make a drink that could stop convulsions,
but she would never kneel and pull the roots,
her own roots beat out of her like silence.
And every spring, and every spring, new footsteps,
and fewer footsteps too, the cemetery growing
across the hill near the pond where now I walk,
the blossoms of the Virginia springbeauty
as vivid as a flower can be growing anywhere,
but especially here on the grounds of the asylum.

RIVER OTTER

The river otter,
sleek and brown,
slips into the marsh
like a legend
I will tell and tell,
after I learn its name,
but for now I watch.

Memorizing its lines,
the way the body moves
from land to sand,
I marvel at this world
where I am never alone
if I let all of life in.

SELFIE AT BIERSTADT'S MT. CORCORAN

Across my right shoulder, your left,
there is a bear approaching a lake
in a panoramic landscape.
Farther still, there is a mountain
honoring the Rocky Mountains
with its composited details
painted from an artist's memories
grander than the West itself.
The mountain, covered in ice,
rises above clouds fraught with light,
one shard piercing the lake like a symbol.
The bear is so small in the grand scheme.
He is there to make us see the glory.
Without him, imagery would pale.

The vast wilderness of that shimmering West
that drew artists to draw what they saw
and also what their vision made them see—
more, something even grander than grand—
makes me want to be part of the painting,
not out front as I am in the selfie, by the bear,
but standing behind a tree in the distance,
only my own imagination visible to the eye.

STONE MOUNTAIN

I know my father could have told me
why sap rises and why it seeps out of trees,
sticky on my fingers when I touch them,
or why a gun shot across a valley
is always louder when you walk alone.

But he isn't here right now, and I am,
a creek's whispers all I have to go on,
and so I listen to what it has to say
about sap and beetles and solitude
and everything else I wonder about
as I wander along this trail, miles to go,
my father's walking stick firm in my hand.

Acknowledgments

About Her: "Gentry Falls"

About Place Journal: "Lesson, Big Laurel Creek"

Artemis: "The Alchemy of Bird Nests," "Rachel When I Am Old," "Showy Orchid on the Virginia Creeper Trail"

Floyd Moonshine: "Loose Strife"

Mason Street Review: "Mockingbird, Smyth Chapel Road"

Mountains Piled Upon Mountains. Appalachian Nature Writing in the Anthropocene (ed. Jessica Cory, WVU Press, 2019): "Landscape with Shoes, Stewarts Creek"

Pendora: "A Love Poem for My Son at Wilburn Ridge"

Pensive: A Global Journal of Spirituality & the Arts: "Millipede"

Pinyon Poetry: "Lewis Fork Wilderness"

Presence. A Journal of Catholic Poetry: "Bristle Cone Pine Tree, Colorado"

Sage of Consciousness Literary Review: "In One Sitting, Jefferson National Forest"

The Southern Poetry Anthology, Volume IX: Virginia (ed. William Wright, J. Bruce Fuller, Amy Wrights, and Jesse Graves, Texas Review Press, 2022): "A Love Poem for My Son at Wilburn Ridge"

Surprised by Joy. A Wising Up Anthology (ed. Charles D. Brockett and Heather Tosteson, Wising Up Press, 2019): "By the Clinch River, St. Paul"

Waltzing with Horses (Poems by Felicia Mitchell, Press 53): "Stone Mountain"

Waves: A Confluence of Women's Voices Online Anthology (A Room of Her Own Foundation, 2024): "The Tattoo I Did Not Get"

Whirlwind: "Wild Grapes Near Saltville"

About the Author

Felicia Mitchell was born in South Carolina and spent her childhood there and on the coast of North Carolina with her parents John A. and Audrey Mitchell and three brothers (John Henry, Charles, Graeme). Following graduation from Booker T. Washington High School in Columbia, she received BA and MA from the University of South Carolina. After completing a PhD at The University of Texas at Austin in 1987, she moved to southwestern Virginia, where she currently resides. Felicia taught English, including creative writing, at Emory & Henry College for many years before retiring with emeritus status. Her scholarly work includes *Her Words: Diverse Voices in Contemporary Women's Poetry*. Poetry collections include *A Mother Speaks, A Daughter Listens: Journeying Together with Dementia* and *Waltzing with Horses*. In recent years, she has blogged about cancer survivorship for *Cure Today*. She volunteers with the Mt. Rogers Appalachian Trail Club and hikes often solo or with friends, including Second Sunday Ramblers and a lifelong friend referenced in "Blue-eyed Mary, My Old Friend."

SELECTED BOOKS FROM WISING UP PRESS

FICTION

My Name Is Your Name & Other Stories
Kerry Langan

Germs of Truth
The Philosophical Transactions of Maria van Leeuwenhoek
Heather Tosteson

Not Native: Short Stories of Immigrant Life in an In-Between World
Murali Kamma

Something Like Hope & Other Stories
William Cass

MEMOIR

My Brother Speaks in Dreams: Of Family, Beauty, and Belonging
Catherine Anderson

Journeys with a Thousand Heroes: A Child Oncologist's Story
John Graham-Pole

Keys to the Kingdom: Reflections on Music and the Mind
Kathleen L. Housley

Last Flight Out: Living, Loving & Leaving
Phyllis A. Langton

POETRY

Source Notes: Seventh Decade
Heather Tosteson

A Hymn that Meanders
Maria Nazos

Epiphanies
Kathleen L. Housley

A Mother Speaks, A Daughter Listens: Journeying
Together Through Dementia
Felicia Mitchell

PLAYS

Trucker Rhapsody & Other Plays
Toni Press-Coffman

WISING UP ANTHOLOGIES

ILLNESS & GRACE: TERROR & TRANSFORMATION

FAMILIES: *The Frontline of Pluralism*

LOVE AFTER 70

DOUBLE LIVES, REINVENTION & THOSE WE LEAVE BEHIND

VIEW FROM THE BED: VIEW FROM THE BEDSIDE

SHIFTING BALANCE SHEETS:
Women's Stories of Naturalized Citizenship & Cultural Attachment

COMPLEX ALLEGIANCES:
Constellations of Immigration, Citizenship & Belonging

DARING TO REPAIR: *What Is It, Who Does It & Why?*

CONNECTED: *What Remains As We All Change*

CREATIVITY & CONSTRAINT

SIBLINGS: *Our First Macrocosm*

THE KINDNESS OF STRANGERS

SURPRISED BY JOY

CROSSING CLASS: *The Invisible Wall*

RE-CREATING OUR COMMON CHORD

GOODNESS

FLIP SIDES:
Truth, Fair Play & Other Myths We Choose to Live By

ADULT CHILDREN:
Being One, Having One & What Goes In-Between

WHOLENESS

OUT OF LINE: WHO DEFINES?
Halfs, Steps, In-Laws & Belonging